Contents

More from Little Cutie on page 6

BY ROBIN ETHERINGTON & ZAK SIMMONDS-HURN

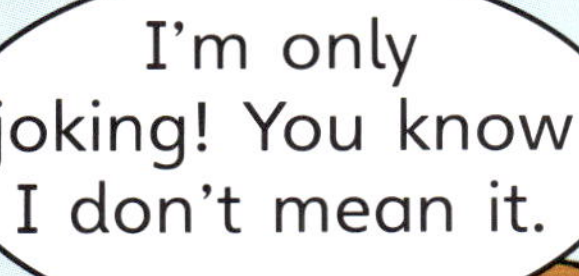

HA HA!
HEE HEE!

Stop laughing, Robbo. I'm serious.
You're serious?
You've just been hit by the biggest ever poop and you're serious? Ha ha ha!

I said, BE QUIET!
THUMP

Woah!
W-W-W-W-WAH!!

Well, that was odd.
Odd?! What happened?

No idea! But you've gone a bit funny.
Let me help you up...

YAAAAH!
Oops!

I don't believe it... I did that. That was ME!

To find out what else Sarah Loopkin gets up to, turn to page 14.

Ooh, such lovely earrings, Brenda!
Thank you...
Little Cutie!
Nice of you to notice.
Heh heh heh hee!
By Gary Northfield
That's weird. I didn't know Charlie noticed things like earrings.
Oh, he often notices mine.
Gasp! Really!
Are you joking?
Lend me some of your jewels!
SHAKE!
SHAKE!
All right.
RATTLE!
Gag!
And so...
Brenda, you have such a lovely collection.
Thank you!
What a beautiful tiara! It goes so well with my bow.
Are you sure I can borrow these?
Of course.
You don't have to wear it all, though!
Oh, don't worry! I really want Charlie to notice me!
Imagine if Charlie liked my jewellery!
I'm giddy with excitement!
There he is!
Oh, Charlie! Charlie!
SPLISH!
SPLISH!
Look at me!
Help! I'm sinking!
SPLOSH!
SPLASH!
My jewels are dragging me down!
Um. What are we meant to be looking at?
Her underwater swimming skills?
Lovely earrings!
Oh, be quiet.

violet
Story and art: Emma Vieceli
Colours: Traci Hui

BEEEP!

CLIK
Hi! I'm Violet. Nice to meet you.
YAAAAAAWN

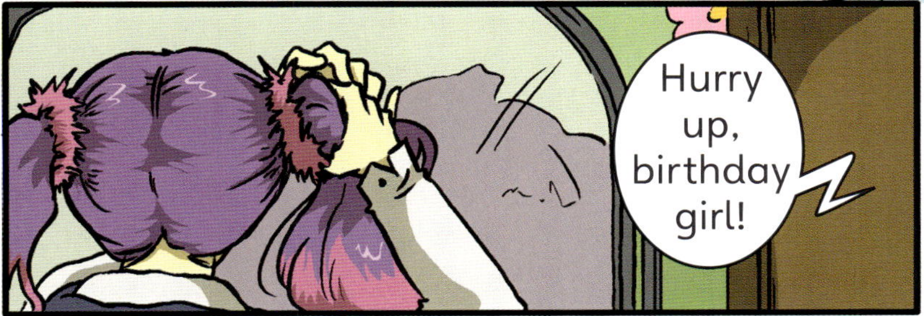
Hurry up, birthday girl!

That's Rose and Gentian, my brother and sister.
Morning, Violet.
Happy Birthday, Shrimp.

Wow, thanks!

Mum and Dad were so wild about flowers.
They named all of us after flowers they loved.

My parents aren't here now, but we're okay.
FLOWER CAFÉ
TOYS
TOYS!
Rose and Gentian look after the Flower Café. Mum and Dad left it to us.

You may be wondering what's so interesting about me.
ER CAFÉ
CLOSED.
SNAP!

You see that? That was the first clue that I got.

VELCRO STRAPS

Argh!

SMASH!

And...

That was when I knew...

...that everything was going to change.

I had super-strength. But it had to be a secret!
RIIIING
At school the next day...
Vernes Locker
What happened to you, Verne?
Oh... I just tripped.
How can someone so clever be so clumsy?
Who knows?
Come on. We've got to go.
RIIIING
Later that day...
CRASH
Where's the homework you said I could copy?
I haven't finished it. Please leave me alone.
Bring it to me tomorrow.

!

Sigh

RIIIIING

Wooooooo

Wooo! I am the spirit of bullied children!
I will make you pay if you don't stop bullying!

Don't be silly. You're just some kid playing a stupid trick.
Woooo! If I were a kid...

...could I do...

...this?
Gah!

OK, I'm sorry! I'll never bully anyone again! Go away!

Hee hee!
Wooo!
That showed him!

The next day...
...I met Cassie and Verne at the fair. It was hard not telling them about my super-strength.

I want candy floss!
Oooh, a big wheel!
Roll up, roll up!
Test your strength!
Only the strongest child will win...

...this cuddly bear.
grand prize!

Oooh!

Oooh!

I'd love that bear!

I'll try my best!

Good luck!

DING
DING

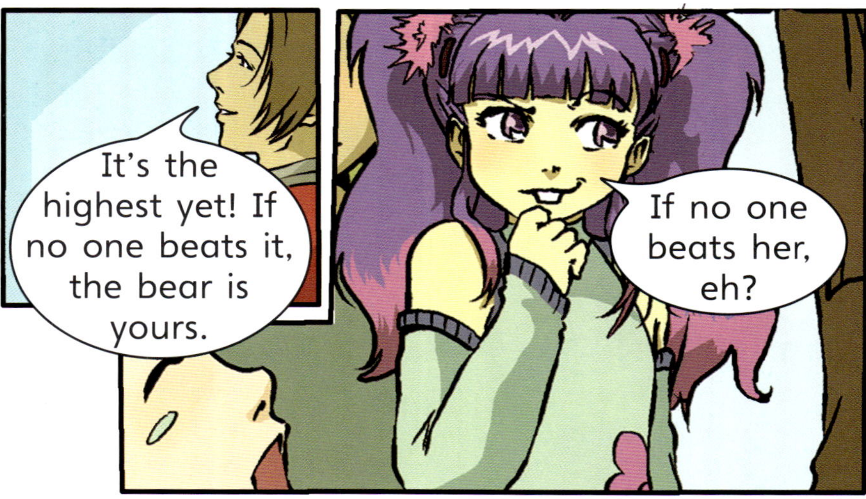
It's the highest yet! If no one beats it, the bear is yours.
If no one beats her, eh?

I'd like to try, please.

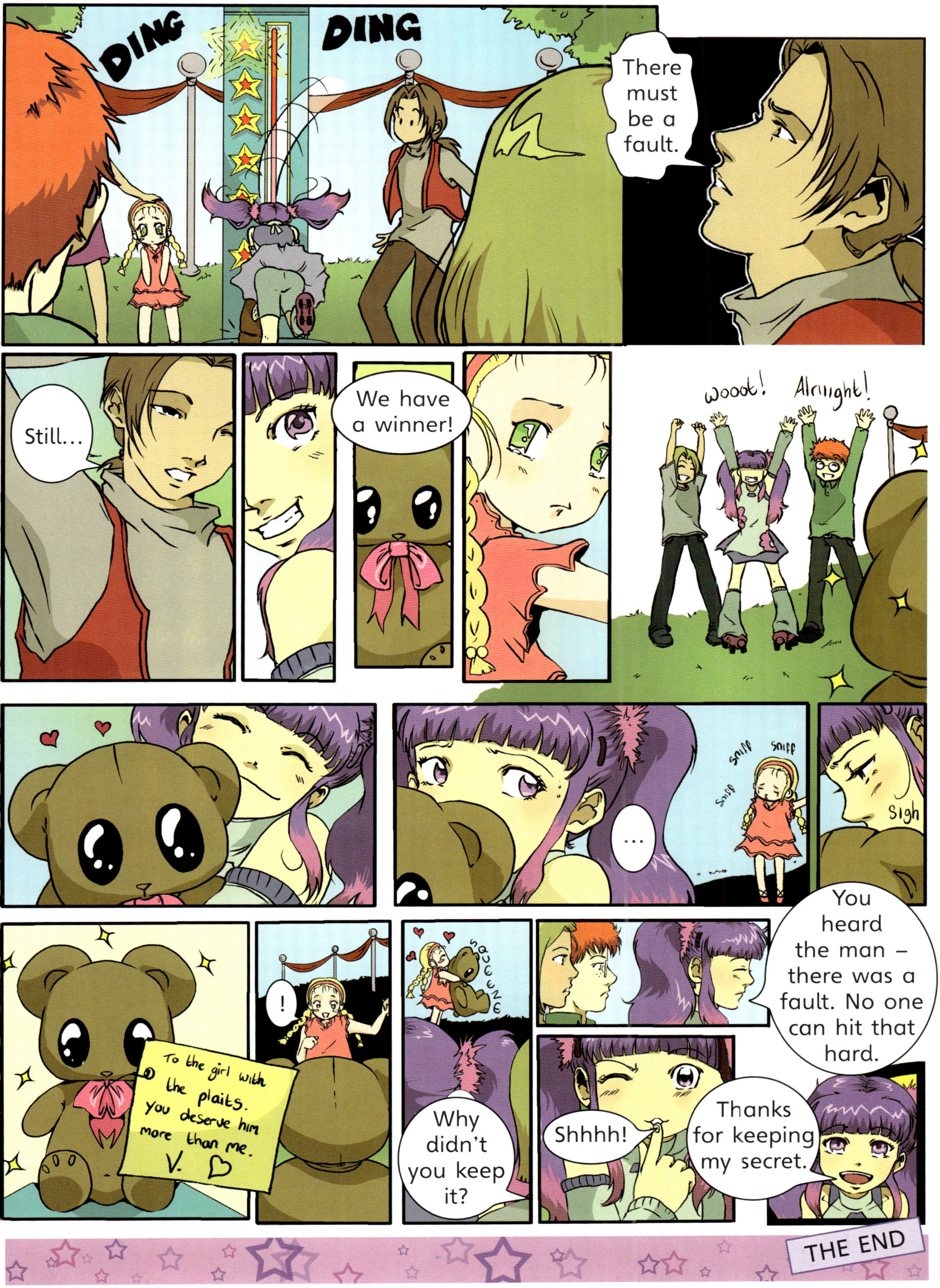

DING

DING

There must be a fault.

Still...

We have a winner!

Woooot! Alright!

You heard the man – there was a fault. No one can hit that hard.

THE END

THE STRANGE, STRANGE WORLD OF WEIRD!
BY ROBIN ETHERINGTON & ZAK SIMMONDS-HURN

Sarah Loopkin has discovered she has 'shocking' powers. Now she's getting her own back.
Lucy Peters! I know it was you who took the photo of me after I got stung on the nose by that bee. But it's time to forgive and forget.
Your nose was as big as a house! You're funny, Sar–

KZZZZT
AH-AH-AHHHHH!
Sarah seems to be enjoying herself, Snarf... she's out of control!

But how did Sarah get this power? She was perfectly normal when we got here.
It was the bird poop.
Of course!
I knew it.

KZZZT
Quick! Over there!

This pigeon has been sitting on that cable for years, soaking up the power. How can we get it to...?
WOOF!
WOOF!

SQUAWK
Snarf, you're a genius! You've...
PHOOT

...done it. YUCK.
Hee hee

Sorry to do this, but I've got to check whether it's worked.
Uh-oh.

Yeah!
YELP!

Meanwhile...
I know you don't want me on the team since I got injured during the cup final. But can't we be friends?
As long as you admit that it was all your fault.
Oh dear, is this my fault too?

Ha ha! I'll never get bored with this!

Come on, Snarf, this is no time for a nap! We've got to save Sarah.
And I know just how.
Ruff
KZEET

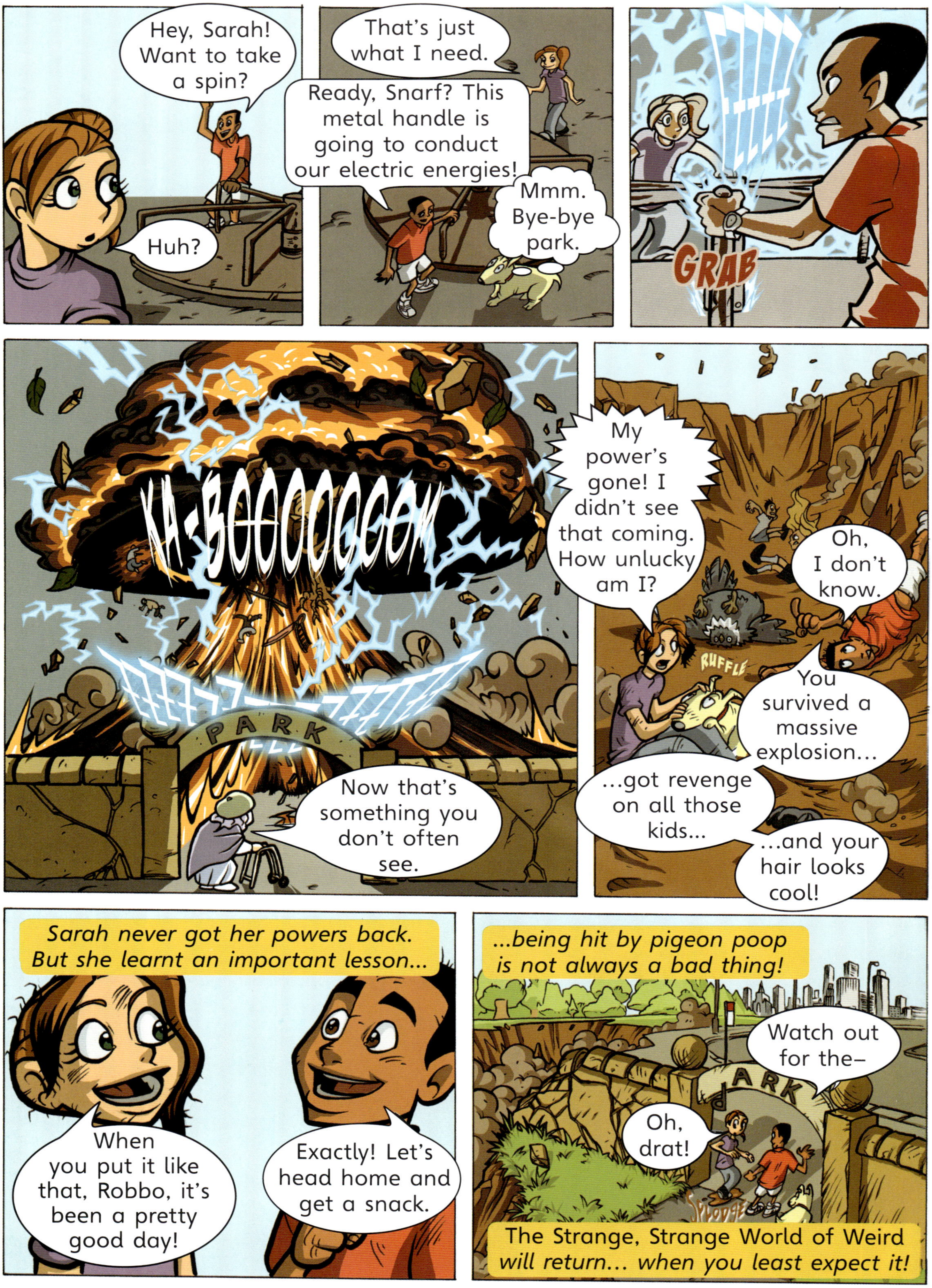

PARK

Now that's something you don't often see.

My power's gone! I didn't see that coming. How unlucky am I?

Oh, I don't know.

RUFFLE

You survived a massive explosion...

...got revenge on all those kids...

...and your hair looks cool!

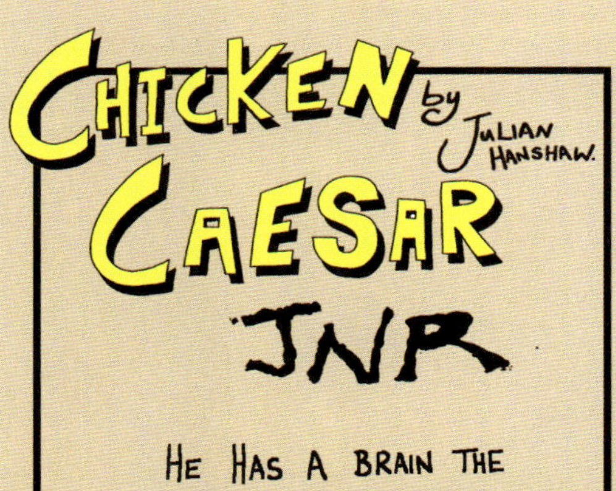

More of Chicken Caesar Jnr on page 24.

ARE GIANT MONSTERS REAL?
That's a good question. First of all, do monsters of any size exist? Well, that depends on what you mean by 'monster'.
Some might say I'm a monster, but I think I'm rather friendly, don't you?
People have been thrilled by the idea of huge creatures for a long time. It started long before movies such as *King Kong*.
That makes me wonder if, long ago, there actually were giant monsters. Maybe all the stories have a kernel of truth in them after all...

The Cyclops, a one-eyed giant, appears in Greek myths. Some believe the idea started when people found the skulls of dwarf elephants. The hole for the trunk was thought to be one gigantic eye socket.

Dragons may be the best known giant monsters in the world.

But are they real?

Well, Komodo Dragons are certainly real. They have been known to eat animals as large as water buffalo.

They grow to about 3 metres long. Big? Yes. Giant? Not really...

Perhaps people found dinosaur bones and thought that they belonged to dragons.

After all, some dinosaurs even had wings like dragons.

But were dinosaurs as big as the giant monsters we see in movies? Hardly. The fearsome T-Rex was only about 6 metres tall.

Some believe that the mighty Seismosaurus was seven times longer than this, but that would have included its tail. Besides, it ate only plants, so it was not very monster-like.

There was no such comfort for the sailors of long ago. They lived in fear that they might end up a meal for...

...a sea serpent!

Were tales of such creatures based on sightings of giant squids?

Thought to grow up to 18 metres, a live giant squid was not even captured or photographed until recently.

Tentacles wrap around their victims. Each one has little cups with its own teeth.

Hunting where there is no light, the giant squid relies on it having the largest eyes in the world.

It certainly sounds like a monster, doesn't it?

For years, much of the proof that giant squids existed came from sperm whales. How?

They were discovered as meals in the whales' bellies.

So maybe whales were the original 'sea monsters'…

One problem with that. The largest animal in the world, the blue whale, is a gentle giant.

Makes one wonder…

Why does the thought of any giant creature scare us? Just because something is big doesn't mean that it's dangerous, does it?

After all, a giant bunny doesn't sound so bad, does it?

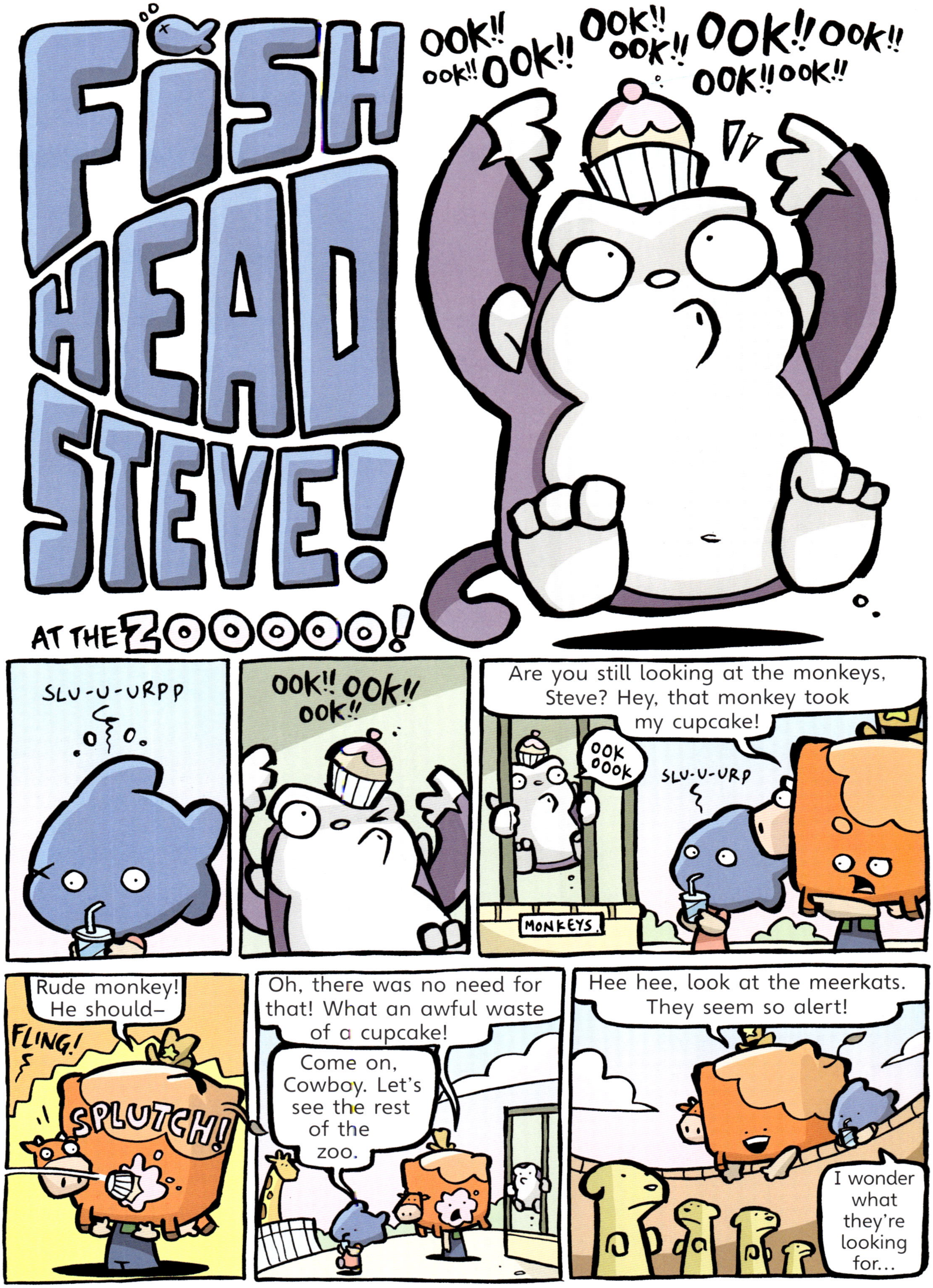

FISH HEAD STEVE!

AT THE ZOOOOOO!

OOK!! ook!! OOK!! OOK!! OOK!! OOK!! OOK!! OOK!! OOK!!

Oh, no! It's food they want! My milkshake!
GRAB!
EERKATS.
Well, when you've finished feeding them, come join me.
BABY ELEPHANTS
MOOF!
What's that, Cow? Do you want to say hello to the baby elephant?
Aww.
Honnk.
Moof.
Moof.
Hee Hee!
SNUGGLES!
Oh, hello, Mr Giraffe! How are you?
SNIFF SNIFF
Hee Hee! It's nature coming together!
And stuff!
Or is it the chocolate in my pocket they're both after?
SQUEEEZE!
CHOMP!!
Uh-oh.
Arrghh! I don't like it! I don't like it!
STREEEETCH!
Run, Cowboy, run! Animals are crazy!
Yes, I know!
CHOMP!!
That's it, Cow, fight back! They can't just attack visitors!
In fact, let's end this visit!
Okay with me, but where should we run to?!
SPRINT!!
A quiet library ... but first, more food!
Agreed!
CHOMP CHOMP CHOMP

The very tip of a very large trifle!
CHICKEN CAESAR JNR
by Julian Hanshaw.
He has a brain the size of a Brussel sprout.
Keep your eyes closed a little longer...
"...you can look now, Jnr!"
Ta Da!
Wow!
I thought you would like it, Jnr. It's for a TV show tonight. I was asked to make the world's biggest cherry trifle!
Nice!
All it needs is a cherry on top. Will you place it there?
Whhiir
Whirrrr
MMM
Count me in!
POP
Place it gently, Jnr. The trifle has only just set.
Remember– gently, Jnr... Very gently.
SHAKE
Later, on TV...
Why am I wearing the trifle? Well, let's say there was an incident in the kitchen...